SAINT DAVID

Patron Saint of Wales

Lois Rock

Illustrated by Finola Stack

Who Was David?

David was a real person in Welsh history. He was a monk, and as a young man he travelled from place to place telling people about Jesus and setting up new monasteries. He is best remembered for the monastery he set up in a faraway corner of south-west Wales, at a place known long ago as Menevia. At the time, David was the

This stained–glass picture shows David dressed as a bishop. A dove, the sign of God's Holy Spirit, is flying towards him.

leader of the church in Wales, so his monastery became an important centre for the church. Long after the time of David, new buildings were added. Today, there is a large and strongly built cathedral at the same place – the place that is now called St Davids.

St Davids Cathedral, where a casket of David's remains are kept safe to this day.

David: An Inspiration to Others

Even as the monks at David's monastery mourned the death of their leader, they knew that the story of his life could inspire others to holy living. He had founded their community and had set them an example of living lives bare of all luxury but rich in holiness.

Stories of David were told aloud and eventually written down by hand in books of leather. Today we know for certain that, just 200 years after David's time, his name was included in a list of saints. Some 300 years after that, the son of the bishop of St Davids wrote a story of the saint's life, using the best information he could find. No one knows if the stories he told were exactly true or if they had been changed over long years of retelling. Later accounts of David's life may have been changed even further. However, all the writers tried to be faithful to the old stories, and the ones that remain for people to read today add up to a picture of David as a gentle and holy man.

David chose to live in a remote place on the coast of Wales.

David the Water-Drinker

AVID WAS A PRINCE, born to a royal family. His father, Sanctus, was the son of Ceredig, prince of Ceredigion in south-west Wales, and his mother, Non, was the daughter of a local chieftain. It was said that his family had a noble ancestry, and that David was related to the famous King Arthur.

When he was a young man, David left home to go and study under a highly respected teacher named Paulinus. The teacher was growing old and, to his great sadness, he was going blind. He asked all his pupils to try to cure him, but none was able to do so. Then David touched the old man's eyes and, by a miracle, he was able to see clearly again.

Paulinus recognized that his kind and eager student was also a sincere Christian and he helped him learn a great deal about the Christian faith. Eventually David decided to devote his life to God. Together with his trusted companions, he became a missionary, travelling the hills and valleys where Wales and England meet. He helped people understand more about the Christian faith and how to live as followers of Jesus.

Wherever he went he was eager to set up monasteries. Here, men lived in communities and dedicated themselves to worshipping God and to farming the land so as to provide for themselves and to help those in need.

On one occasion, David left his homeland to travel with two companions to Jerusalem – to the very city where Jesus had died and where his followers claimed he rose again. The leader of the church there greeted them warmly. He saw that David was a true man of God and commanded him to work hard to protect the Christian faith. He sent David gifts to encourage him in his work: an altar, a bell, a tunic woven with gold and a staff.

Tales were told that these gifts were blessed by God and could work miracles for anyone who touched them.

In time, David wanted to find a place where he could settle down. One day, David and his companions were in the corner of south-west Wales. A chilly wind blew, bringing grey drenching rain in from the ocean. Weeds and grasses sprouted among the many rocky outcrops.

'Let us build our community here, far from all the busy things of this world,' said David.

The companions were not surprised at this. For years David had ruled that the monks in his monasteries should live simple, frugal lives. He taught them that self-discipline in everyday things would help them to live righteously. Here, in this remote place, they would cultivate the thin soil, pulling the plough themselves to prepare the land for crops.

'We can grow grain to make bread,' he said, 'and also a few vegetables that will survive the cold sea

breezes – leeks and onions, for example. We only drink water.' David himself was already nicknamed 'the Water-Drinker'.

'But the stream here is not good,' the monks warned him. 'People say that in summer it is only a trickle.'

David went to the place where it flowed and prayed to God. By a miracle, it became a spring of pure, clear water.

So the building began there, at Menevia. The monks worked in silence, for David wanted them to learn always to think about their faith and to pray to God.

The novices found the training hard. 'Why are you yawning?' David asked a young monk sharply.

'I am not used to such short nights,' came the reply. 'And although I know that Our Lord Jesus was in the tomb from Friday evening till Sunday morning, must we stay awake all that time every week?'

'Do not give in to yourself,' David encouraged him. 'I have trained myself to stay awake in prayer many nights.'

The monk nodded humbly. It was true that David seemed to be able to force himself to do anything. Why, he even spent long hours standing up to his neck in icy water reciting aloud from the Bible and never once complaining!

David was not so strict with people outside the community. The work the monks did enabled them to be generous with the poor people who lived nearby and to provide meals and lodgings for pilgrims and travellers.

One day, there was a great meeting
of church people at a place called
Llanddewi Brefi. They wanted
to choose a new leader for
the church in Wales –
someone whose faith
was strong and who had
true understanding of it.
    The place was thronged.
Everyone wanted to
speak and no one could
be heard. Even when
they chose a mound
and made a pile
of clothing
for speakers
to stand
on, still

there was no one whose voice would carry.

Old Paulinus was in the crowd. 'Send for David,' he urged. 'I know him to be wise.'

David had not wanted to put himself forward as the new leader. However, he was at last persuaded to come. He took his place on the mound of clothing and prayed to God. A white dove, the sign of God's Holy Spirit, came and sat on his shoulder. Then, when he spoke, everyone listened and was convinced of his wisdom.

It was soon agreed that David should be the new leader of the church.

David led the people wisely, but he refused to lord it over them. Instead, he continued to live as a monk in Menevia. One Sunday, he stood up to preach the sermon. 'Be joyful. Keep the faith. Follow the example I have set, and do the little things that you have seen me do.'

The following Tuesday, 1 March, David died.

A Prayer Inspired by Saint David

*D*ear God,

Help us to turn away from the busy things of this world and to think more about your love and goodness.

Help us to work hard and to live simply so we are able to help others.

Help us to remember to serve one another, and to do the little things that make such a difference.

Saint David's Day

David was made a saint by the pope in Rome in the year 1120, and his special day was declared to be 1 March, out of respect for the day he died.

His monastery in Menevia, St Davids, became a place of pilgrimage, where Christians would travel to spend more time thinking about their faith. Some came hoping for a miracle, for David's remains were there, and it was believed that their holiness could cure illness.

Today, 1 March is celebrated in Wales as a national festival. The national emblems – leeks and daffodils – are worn pinned to clothing. Many school children wear national dress, the style of which dates back from a couple of centuries ago! For girls, a tall beaver hat with a glimpse of a lace frill from the bonnet underneath is very popular indeed.

Wales is sometimes known as the land of song, and all over Wales and in Welsh communities throughout the world there are music festivals to honour Saint David's Day. This kind of festival is called an Eisteddfod. It will include traditional Welsh songs and, wherever possible, music played on the Welsh harp. There may also be poetry recitals and storytelling in Welsh to celebrate this ancient language.

Welsh girls in national costume for Saint David's Day

Index

Text by Lois Rock
Illustrations copyright © 2005 Finola Stack
This edition copyright © 2005 Lion Hudson

The moral rights of the author and illustrator have been asserted

A Lion Children's Book
an imprint of
Lion Hudson plc
Mayfield House, 256 Banbury Road,
Oxford OX2 7DH, England
www.lionhudson.com
ISBN 0 7459 4809 X

First edition 2005
10 9 8 7 6 5 4 3 2 1 0

A catalogue record for this book is available from the British Library

Typeset in 15/20 Revival565 BT
Printed and bound in Singapore

Picture Acknowledgments
Front cover: The Photolibrary Wales
The Photolibrary Wales: pp. 4, 5, 6–7, 21